D0310404

What Can Live at the Beach

John-Paul Wilkins

Raintree

Raintree is an imprint of Capstone Global Library Limited, a company incorporated in England and Wales having its registered office at 7 Pilgrim Street, London, EC4V 6LB – Registered company number: 6695582

www.raintreepublishers.co.uk
myorders@raintreepublishers.co.uk

Text © Capstone Global Library Limited 2015
First published in hardback in 2014
The moral rights of the proprietor have been asserted.

Edited by Diyan Leake and Gina Kammer
Designed by Cynthia Akiyoshi
Picture research by Elizabeth Alexander and Tracy Cummins
Production by Victoria Fitzgerald
Originated by Capstone Global Library Ltd
Printed and bound in China by Leo Paper Group

ISBN 978 1 406 28500 0
18 17 16 15 14
10 9 8 7 6 5 4 3 2 1

British Library Cataloguing in Publication Data
A full catalogue record for this book is available from the British Library.

Acknowledgements
We would like to thank the following for permission to reproduce photographs:
 Alamy: © Alex Bramwell, front cover, © Arterra Picture Library, 19, © Robert HENNO, 17; Corbis: © Darlyne A. Murawski/National Geographic Society, 15; iStockphoto: © Andreas Altenburger, 12, © coastalrunner, 7, © towlake, 14; Shutterstock: BarryTuck, 20, 23c, Chabaphoto, 10, holbox, 11, 23e, Jung Hsuan, 22, kajornyot, 6, loraart8, 5, Masahiro Suzuki, 21, Noel Powell, 4, 23b, back cover left, Omega77, 18, 23a, raulbaenacasado, 16, Sally Wallis, 8, back cover right, Tomek Friedrich, 13, 23f, Vladimirs Koskins, 9, 23d.

Every effort has been made to contact copyright holders of material reproduced in this book. Any omissions will be rectified in subsequent printings if notice is given to the publisher.

Contents

Some words are shown in bold, **like this**. You can find out what they mean by looking in the glossary.

What is a beach habitat?

A **habitat** is a place where animals or plants live. A beach is a habitat.

Habitats provide food and **shelter** for the things that live there.

A beach is an area of land next to the sea.
Beaches are often covered in sand or stones.

Animals and plants have special features to
live on beaches.

How do plants live on beaches?

Plants on beaches need to protect themselves from strong winds and salt from seawater.

Salt sucks up water and dries things out. If you watered a normal plant with seawater, it would die.

Sea campion grows on rocky beaches.

The leaves of sea campion are close together like a carpet to protect it from the wind.

The thick, shiny leaves of sea kale help protect it from salty seawater.

Its long roots can take in freshwater from deep underground.

Some plants can help shape the land
on beaches.
The roots of marram grass hold sand **dunes**
together and stop them from blowing away.

How can plants help animals on beaches?

Plants are very important for beach **habitats**. They provide food and **shelter** for many animals.

Many plants provide a home for small animals.

These plants are called **microhabitats**.

A microhabitat is a very small habitat within a larger habitat.

How do animals make homes on beaches?

Lugworms live in burrows in the sand. They create their burrows by eating the sand and pooing it out as they go.

Bristles at the head end help lugworms keep a good grip as they burrow.

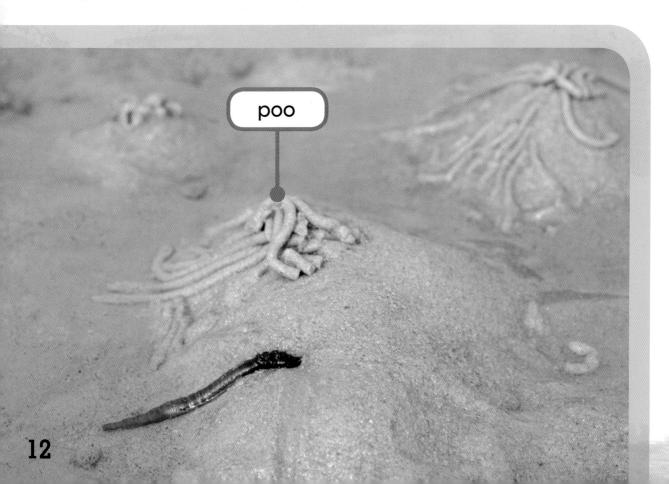

poo

barnacles

A barnacle's home is its shell. The shell protects it from **predators** and provides **shelter** from hot and cold weather.

Barnacles make a special glue to stick themselves to rocks on seashores.

How do animals feed on beaches?

Starfish live in rock pools on beaches. A rock pool is a **microhabitat**.

The starfish uses tiny suckers on its arms to open the shells of small shellfish. Then it eats the shellfish inside.

Dog whelks use a special mouth part to drill a hole in the shells of mussels and barnacles.

They squirt juices into the hole that turn the mussel into liquid. Then the dog whelk sucks it up!

Stilts have long legs, so they can walk in shallow water to find food.

Their long, thin beaks help them search for food in mud and sand.

An antlion baby makes a clever trap to catch food. It digs a pit in the sand and buries itself at the bottom of it.

When an ant or other small animal falls in, the antlion gobbles it up!

How do animals hide on beaches?

Ghost crabs live on sandy beaches. They only come out at night.

Ghost crabs' sandy colour helps them to **blend in** and stay hidden from **predators**.

Sand fleas' powerful legs help them dig burrows in the sand.

To stay hidden, sand fleas plug the tops of their burrows with sand. They come out to feed when it is dark.

How do animals protect themselves on beaches?

Sea urchins can be found clinging to rocks in some rock pools.

Sea urchins have spines all over their bodies to protect them from **predators**.

Hermit crabs use the shells of dead animals, such as whelks, to protect their soft bodies.

As they grow, they find bigger shells to live in.

That's amazing!

Sea cucumbers can be found in some shallow waters and in tide pools. They can squeeze through the tightest of spaces.

Sea cucumbers just change their bodies as if their insides are liquid, and flow on through!

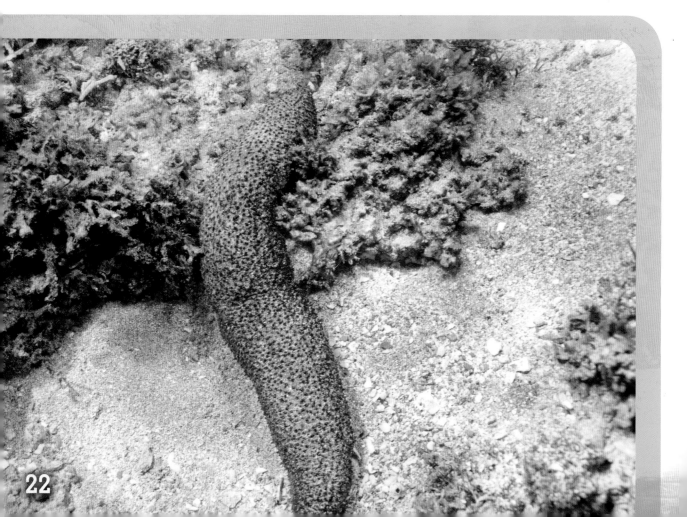

Picture glossary

 **blend in** to mix together with surroundings

 **dune** a mound of sand built up by the wind

 **habitat** a place where an animal or plant lives

 **microhabitat** a very small habitat within a larger habitat

 **predator** an animal that hunts other animals for food

 **shelter** a place that protects from danger or bad weather

Find out more

Books

Fleming, Sarah. *Save Our Coasts!* (Oxford University Press, 2005)

Ganeri, Anita. *Exploring Coasts: A Benjamin Blog and His Inquisitive Dog Investigation.* (Raintree, 2014)

Websites

www.wildlifewatch.org.uk/explore-wildlife
Under "Habitats" click on "Beaches and coasts."

www.animalfactguide.com
Search interesting facts about beach animals.

Index